How to Use The Write & Draw Travel Journal

Use this journal to get the most out of your travels by writing your journal and recording sketches/stick photos on the same page

- Journalling
- Sketching
- Photo Album
- Stick Mementos

Made in the USA
Middletown, DE
08 December 2019